SOAR TO SUCCESS

THE INTERMEDIATE
INTERVENTION PROGRAM

Student Guide

Level 4

Senior Author

J. David Cooper

Authors

Irene Boschken

Janet McWilliams

Lynne Pistochini

 HOUGHTON MIFFLIN

Boston • Atlanta • Dallas • Denver • Geneva, Illinois • Palo Alto • Princeton

Design, Production, and Illustration: PiperStudiosInc

Printed in the U.S.A.

ISBN: 0-395-78132-9

16 17 18 19 20-WC-04 03 02 01

SOAR TO SUCCESS

Contents

SOAR TO SUCCESS

Name _____

REFLECTION

1 How do you think Agnes and Clarence felt after Clarence lost his job and the bank took their house?

_____

_____

_____

_____

_____

REFLECTION

2 Do you think it is a good idea for the family to leave for Idaho? Why or why not?

_____

_____

_____

_____

_____

Potato

Name _____

Circle the strategy you used most.

Strategy Box			
Predict	Summarize	Clarify	Question

Name at least one place where you used this strategy. Write the page number(s).

_____

_____

How did this strategy help you?

_____

_____

_____

_____

_____

_____

Name _____

REFLECTION

4

Why do you think the author wrote this story?

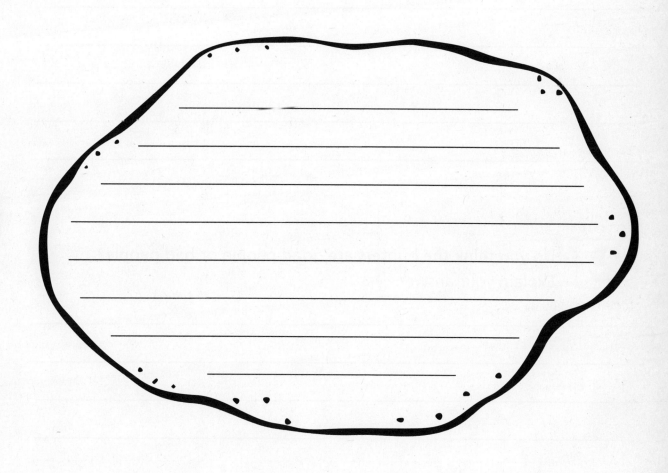

Tippu

Name _____

REFLECTION

1

Do you think the stork will help the animals find a safe place? Why or why not?

_____

_____

_____

_____

_____

REFLECTION

2

Do you think the hunters are good people or bad people? Explain your answer.

_____

_____

_____

_____

_____

Name _____

REFLECTION

3

Circle the strategy you used most.

Strategy Box			
Predict	Summarize	Clarify	Question

Name at least one place where you used this strategy or modeled it for someone else. Write the page number(s).

_____

_____

_____

How did this strategy help you?

_____

_____

_____

_____

_____

_____

_____

Tippu

Name _____

4

What do you think Tippu learned about people?

_____

_____

_____

_____

_____

_____

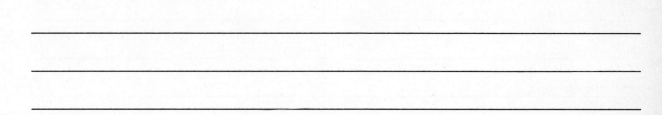

Name _____

REFLECTION

1

Why do you think the narrator's family cannot agree on a name for the cat?

_____

_____

_____

_____

REFLECTION

2

Do you think the cat should be named as soon as possible? Why or why not?

_____

_____

_____

_____

Name _____

Circle the strategy you used most.

Strategy Box			
Predict	Summarize	Clarify	Question

Name at least one place where you used this strategy or modeled it for someone else. Write the page number(s).

_____

_____

_____

How did this strategy help you?

_____

_____

_____

_____

_____

_____

Name _____

REFLECTION

4   Do you think the name Lucky fits the cat? Why or why not?

_____

_____

_____

_____

_____

_____

Name _____

REFLECTION

1

How do you think Arthur felt at the end of the day when all the rabbits had been sold?

_____

_____

_____

_____

_____

_____

REFLECTION

2

Why does Arthur practice so hard to be like a fish?

_____

_____

_____

_____

_____

Name _____

REFLECTION

3

Do you think Arthur is an ordinary dog? Why or why not?

_____

_____

_____

_____

_____

Name _____

REFLECTION

4

Circle the section you liked best in *Who Wants Arthur?*

Pages 6–9
Arthur practices being a rabbit.

Pages 10–23
Arthur practices being a snake, a fish, and other animals.

Pages 24–27
Arthur decides to be an ordinary dog.

Pages 28–30
Arthur finds a home with Melanie and her grandfather.

How did one or more of the four strategies help you read that section?

Predict

_____

_____

Clarify

_____

_____

Summarize

_____

_____

Question

_____

_____

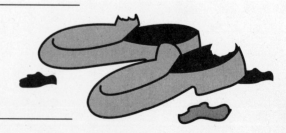

Name _____

My Notes to Clarify

Write any words or ideas that you need to clarify. Include the page numbers.

Words or Ideas	Page
Pages 4–13	
Pages 14–25	
Pages 26–33	
Pages 34–41	
Pages 42–47	

Name _____

REFLECTION

1

Why is the color of a wolf important to where it lives?

_____

_____

_____

_____

_____

_____

REFLECTION

2

Summarize the role of the leader in a wolf pack.

_____

_____

_____

_____

_____

_____

Name _____

REFLECTION

3

Circle the strategy you used most.

Strategy Box			
Predict	Summarize	Clarify	Question

Name at least one place where you used this strategy or modeled it for someone else. Write the page number(s).

_____

_____

_____

_____

_____

How did this strategy help you?

_____

_____

_____

_____

_____

The Wonder of Wolves

Name _____

4

How do wolves hunt for their food?

_____

_____

_____

_____

_____

_____

5

What sounds do wolves make? Why do they make these sounds?

_____

_____

_____

_____

_____

Name _____

Story Map

Title

Setting

Characters

Problem

Major Events

Outcome

Name _____

My Notes to Clarify

Write any words or ideas that you need to clarify. Include the page numbers.

Words or Ideas	Page
Pages 4–11	
Pages 12–17	
Pages 18–23	
Pages 24–32	

Name _____

REFLECTION

How might Grandaddy's advice be helpful to JoJo?

_____

_____

_____

REFLECTION

How might P.J.'s advice be helpful to JoJo?

_____

_____

REFLECTION

3

What sport would you like to visualize yourself doing well?
What would your picture look like?

_____

_____

_____

_____

_____

_____

Name _____

REFLECTION

4

Circle the strategy you used most in *JoJo's Flying Side Kick.*

Strategy Box			
Predict	Clarify	Summarize	Question

1. Describe a place in the story where you used this strategy.

_____

_____

How did this strategy help you read that section?

_____

_____

2. Describe another place in the story where you used this strategy.

_____

_____

How did this strategy help you read that section?

_____

_____

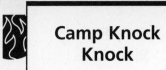 **Camp Knock Knock**

Name _____

Story Map

Title

Setting

Characters

Problem

Major Events

Outcome

Name _____

My Notes to Clarify

Write any words or ideas that you need to clarify. Include the page numbers.

Words or Ideas	Page
Pages 6–13	
Pages 14–23	
Pages 24–33	
Pages 34–42	
Pages 43–47	

Name _____

1

Do you think it was a good idea for Crow and Willie to have a contest? Why or why not?

_____

_____

_____

_____

2

Who do you think tells better knock-knock jokes, Willie or Crow? Explain.

_____

_____

_____

_____

Name _____

REFLECTION

3

Circle the strategy you used most so far.

Strategy Box			
Predict	**Summarize**	**Clarify**	**Question**

Name at least one place where you used this strategy or modeled it for someone else. Write the page number(s).

_____

_____

_____

_____

How did this strategy help you?

_____

_____

_____

_____

Name _____

REFLECTION

4

Do you think the knock-knock contest is fair? Why or why not?

_____

_____

_____

_____

_____

REFLECTION

5

Did Willie and Crow show good sportsmanship after the contest? Explain your answer.

_____

_____

_____

_____

_____

Name _____

Story Map

Title

Setting

Characters

Problem

Major Events

Outcome

Name _____

My Notes to Clarify

Write any words or ideas that you need to clarify. Include the page numbers.

Words or Ideas	Page
Pages 6–17	
Pages 18–29	
Pages 30–43	
Pages 44–53	
Pages 54–63	

Name _____

REFLECTION

1

What would it be like to live in a dugout?

_____

_____

_____

REFLECTION

2

Why did Daddy want the boys to remember the day the Indians brought food?

_____

_____

_____

Name _____

REFLECTION

3 Summarize what the boys did to take care of themselves and Little Brother.

_____

_____

_____

_____

_____

REFLECTION

4 How do you think the boys have changed since coming to Kansas?

_____

_____

_____

Name _____

REFLECTION

5 Circle the section you liked best in *Wagon Wheels*.

Pages 6–17
Building a
dugout

Pages 18–29
Surviving
the winter

Pages 30–43
Daddy leaves
and the
boys stay.

Pages 44–53
Daddy sends
a letter and
the boys
set off.

Pages 54–63
The boys find
Daddy.

How did one or more of the four strategies help you read
that section?

Predict
_____

_____

Summarize
_____

_____

_____

Clarify
_____

_____

_____

Question
_____

_____

_____

Name _____

My Notes to Clarify

Write any words or ideas that you need to clarify. Include the page numbers.

Words or Ideas	Page
Pages 6–17	
Pages 18–27	
Pages 28–37	
Pages 38–45	

Name _____

REFLECTION

1   What are the characteristics of a good visiting dog?

_____

_____

_____

REFLECTION

2   Why did Rosie have to pass a test before she
could become a visiting dog?

_____

_____

_____

Name _____

REFLECTION

3

Why are dogs good companions for sick or elderly people?

_____

_____

_____

_____

Name _____

REFLECTION

Circle the section of the book that you liked best.

Pages 6–17 Introduction to Rosie	**Pages 18–27** Rosie's Training
Pages 28–37 Rosie Visits the Children's Hospital	**Pages 38–45** Rosie Visits a Nursing Home

Circle a strategy that helped you read that part of the book.

Strategy Box			
Predict	**Clarify**	**Summarize**	**Question**

Tell how you used that strategy.

_____

_____

_____

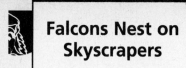

Name _____

K-W-L Chart

Title

What I **K**now	What I **W**ant to Find Out	What I **L**earned

Name _____

My Notes to Clarify

Write any words or ideas that you need to clarify. Include the
page numbers.

Words or Ideas	Page
Pages 4–9	
Pages 10–17	
Pages 18–23	
Pages 24–29	

Name _____

1

Summarize how a falcon hunts for food.

_____

_____

_____

_____

2

Do you think farmers should have sprayed the crops with DDT? Explain.

_____

_____

_____

_____

Name _____

REFLECTION

3 Do you think it is important for people to help and protect birds like the peregrine falcon? Why?

_____

_____

_____

_____

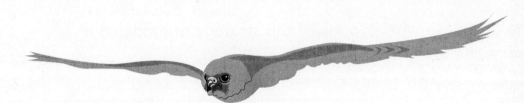

REFLECTION

4

Circle the strategy you used most in *Falcons Nest on Skyscrapers*.

Strategy Box			
Question	Clarify	Summarize	Predict

Name one place where you used this strategy or modeled it for someone else. Write the page number(s).

_____

How did this strategy help you?

_____

_____

Name another place where you used this strategy or modeled it for someone else. Write the page number(s).

_____

How did this strategy help you?

_____

_____

Name _____

Story Map

Title

Setting

Characters

Problem

Major Events

Outcome

Name _____

My Notes to Clarify

Write any words or ideas that you need to clarify. Include the page numbers.

Words or Ideas	Page
Pages 4–11 _____	_____
_____	_____
_____	_____
Pages 12–21 _____	_____
_____	_____
_____	_____
_____	_____
_____	_____
Pages 22–27 _____	_____
_____	_____
_____	_____
_____	_____
Pages 28–32 _____	_____
_____	_____
_____	_____
_____	_____

Name _____

REFLECTION

1 How might the camping trip be a good thing for both Dad and the boy?

_____

_____

REFLECTION

2 Why do you think Dad told the boy that he didn't bring any food?

_____

_____

_____

Name _____

REFLECTION

3

What would you do if you were in the boy's place?
Would you ask Dad to go back to the creek to camp?

_____

_____

Name _____

REFLECTION

4 Circle the strategy you used most in *The Lost Lake.*

Strategy Box			
Predict	**Clarify**	**Summarize**	**Question**

1. Describe a place in the story where you used this strategy.

   _____

   _____

   How did this strategy help you read that section?

   _____

   _____

2. Describe another place in the story where you used this strategy.

   _____

   _____

   How did this strategy help you read that section?

   _____

   _____

Name _____

Semantic Map

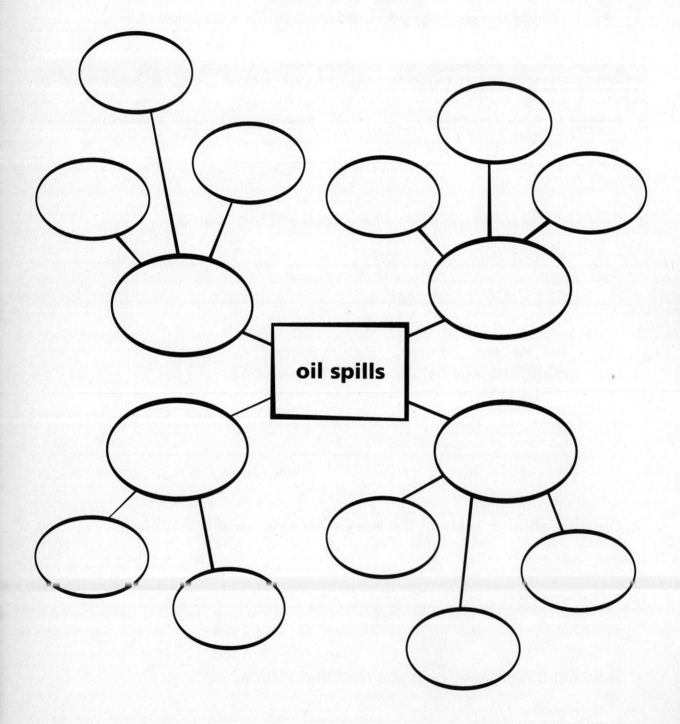

oil spills

Name _____

My Notes to Clarify

Write any words or ideas that you need to clarify. Include the page numbers.

Words or Ideas	Page
Pages 4–13	
Pages 14–23	
Pages 24–29	
Pages 30–32	

REFLECTION

1   What happened to birds and other animals in Alaska as a result of the oil spill?

_____

_____

_____

_____

_____

REFLECTION

2   Summarize one of the different ways people help to clean up oil spills.

_____

_____

_____

_____

_____

_____

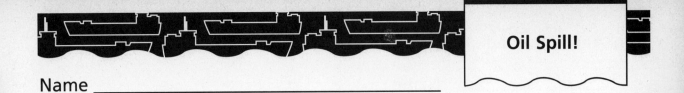

Name _____

REFLECTION

3

Circle your favorite section so far. Then write about how one or more strategies have helped you read that section.

Pages 4–13	Pages 14–23	Pages 24–29
The *Exxon Valdez* disaster	Causes and cleanup at sea	Cleanup on shore

_____

_____

_____

_____

_____

REFLECTION

4

Write a letter you might send to someone in Congress about oil spills.

_____

_____

_____

_____

_____

Name _____

Story Map

Title

Setting

Characters

Problem

Major Events

Outcome

Name _____

My Notes to Clarify

Write any words or ideas that you need to clarify. Include the page numbers.

Words or Ideas	Page
Pages 4–11 _____	_____
_____	_____
_____	_____
Pages 12–17 _____	_____
_____	_____
_____	_____
_____	_____
_____	_____
Pages 18–23 _____	_____
_____	_____
Pages 24–27 _____	_____
_____	_____
Pages 28–32 _____	_____
_____	_____
_____	_____
_____	_____

Amelia's Road

Name _____

Do you think Amelia will find a place to settle down?
Why or why not?

_____

_____

Why do you think Amelia wants to stay at Fillmore
Elementary School? Explain.

_____

_____

_____

Name _____

REFLECTION

3

Circle the strategy you used most in *Amelia's Road.*

Strategy Box			
Predict	Clarify	Summarize	Question

Describe a place in the story where you used this strategy.

_____

_____

How did this strategy help you read that section?

_____

_____

Describe another place in the story where you used this strategy.

_____

_____

How did this strategy help you read that section?

_____

_____

_____

Name _____

REFLECTION

4

Do you think that what Amelia did will make her feel as though she belongs to that place? Why or why not?

_____

_____

_____

REFLECTION

5

How did Amelia feel about leaving? Why did she feel that way?

_____

_____

Name _____

K-W-L Chart

Title

What I **K**now	What I **W**ant to Find Out	What I **L**earned

Name _____

My Notes to Clarify

Write any words or ideas that you need to clarify. Include the page numbers.

Words or Ideas	Page
Pages 4–13	
Pages 14–21	
Pages 22–29	
Pages 30–32	

Name _____

REFLECTION

1

What do bats hunt? Why is this helpful to people?

_____

_____

_____

REFLECTION

2

Do you think people should be afraid of bats?
Why or why not?

_____

_____

_____

_____

Name _____

REFLECTION

3

Do you think it is important for people to help bats?
Why or why not?

_____

_____

_____

_____

Name _____

REFLECTION

4 Circle the strategy you used most in *Zipping, Zapping, Zooming Bats*.

Strategy Box			
Predict	**Summarize**	**Clarify**	**Question**

Name one place where you used this strategy or modeled it for someone else. Write the page number(s).

_____

How did this strategy help you?

_____

_____

Name another place where you used this strategy or modeled it for someone else. Write the page number(s).

_____

How did this strategy help you?

_____

_____

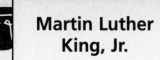

Name _____

Main Ideas and Details

Title _____

1. Main idea _____

  a. Detail _____

  b. _____

  c. _____

  d. _____

2. _____

  a. _____

  b. _____

  c. _____

  d. _____

3. _____

  a. _____

  b. _____

  c. _____

  d. _____

4. _____

  a. _____

  b. _____

  c. _____

  d. _____

Name _____

My Notes to Clarify

Write any words or ideas that you need to clarify. Include the page numbers.

Words or Ideas	Page
Pages 4–11 _____	_____
_____	_____
_____	
Pages 12–17 _____	
_____	_____
_____	
Pages 18–29 _____	_____
_____	
_____	_____
Pages 30–35 _____	_____
_____	
_____	_____
Pages 36–45 _____	_____
_____	_____
_____	
_____	_____

Name _____

REFLECTION

1 How do you think M.L. felt when he couldn't play with his friends anymore?

_____

_____

_____

REFLECTION

2 How do you think Martin felt seeing his teacher looking ready to cry?

_____

_____

Name _____

REFLECTION 3

Circle the strategy you used most in *Martin Luther King, Jr.*

Strategy Box			
Predict	Summarize	Clarify	Question

Describe a place in the story where you used this strategy.

_____

How did this strategy help you read that section?

_____

REFLECTION 4

Why did Martin take Yoki to Funtown?

_____

_____

REFLECTION 5

What do you think was the most important thing that Martin Luther King, Jr. changed? Why?

_____

_____

Name _____

Story Map

Title

Setting

Characters

Problem

Major Events

Outcome

Name _____

My Notes to Clarify

Write any words or ideas that you need to clarify. Include the page numbers.

Words or Ideas	Page
Pages 5–13	
Pages 14–21	
Pages 22–31	
Pages 32–39	
Pages 40–47	

Name _____

REFLECTION

Why did Milton need to use snowshoes outside?

_____

_____

_____

REFLECTION

How do you think Mickey, the grocer's son, felt seeing Milton's snowshoes? Why do you think he felt that way?

_____

_____

_____

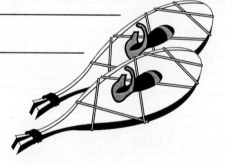

Name _____

3 Circle the strategy you used most so far in *The Snow Walker*.

Strategy Box			
Predict	Summarize	Clarify	Question

Name at least one place where you used this strategy. Write the page number(s).

_____

_____

_____

_____

How did this strategy help you?

_____

_____

_____

_____

_____

_____

REFLECTION

4

Summarize how Milton helped the woman with the sick husband.

_____

_____

_____

_____

REFLECTION

5

What do you think was the scariest thing that happened on Milton's walk home? Why?

_____

_____

_____

_____

_____

Name _____

K-W-L Chart

Title

What I **K**now	What I **W**ant to Find Out	What I **L**earned

Name _____

My Notes to Clarify

Write any words or ideas that you need to clarify. Include the page numbers.

Words or Ideas	Page
Chapter 1: _____	_____
_____	_____
_____	_____
Chapter 2: _____	_____
_____	_____
_____	_____
Chapter 3: _____	_____
_____	_____
_____	_____
Chapter 4: _____	_____
_____	_____
Chapter 5: _____	_____
_____	_____
_____	_____
Chapter 6: _____	_____
_____	_____

Name _____

REFLECTION

1 How are whales different from fish?

_____

_____

_____

_____

_____

REFLECTION

2 Summarize the characteristics of the two main groups
of whales.

_____

_____

_____

_____

_____

Whales

Name _____

3

Circle the chapter that interested you most so far in *Whales.*

Chapter 1
Whales Walked Here

Chapter 2
Do Whales Have
Teeth?

Chapter 3
Whale Families

How did one or more of the four strategies help you read
that chapter?

Predict

_____

_____

Summarize

_____

_____

Clarify

_____

_____

Question

_____

_____

Name _____

REFLECTION

4

What do you think is the most important thing that a humpback calf learns from its mother? Why?

_____

_____

_____

REFLECTION

5

Do you think more should be done to save and study whales? Why or why not?

_____

_____

_____

_____

_____

_____

Story Map

Title

Setting

Characters

Problem

Major Events

Outcome

Name _____

My Notes to Clarify

Write any words or ideas that you need to clarify. Include the page numbers.

Words or Ideas	Page
Pages 1–10 _____	_____
_____	_____
_____	_____
Pages 11–21 _____	_____
_____	_____
_____	_____
Pages 22–30 _____	_____
_____	_____
_____	_____
Pages 31–43 _____	_____
_____	_____
Pages 44–50 _____	_____
_____	_____
Pages 51–59 _____	_____
_____	_____
_____	_____

Name _____

REFLECTION

1

Why was being a good hitter so important to José?

_____

_____

_____

_____

_____

REFLECTION

2

Do you think José's father was being fair to him? _____
Why or why not?

_____

_____

_____

_____

_____

Name _____

Copyright © Houghton Mifflin Company. All rights reserved.

REFLECTION

3 If you were one of José's teammates, what would you say to him about his playing?

_____

_____

_____

_____

_____

_____

REFLECTION

4

Summarize what José does to get the bat and then to lose the bat.

_____

_____

_____

_____

_____

_____

Name _____

REFLECTION

Which strategy do you think would be helpful to use with
Centerfield Ballhawk?

Strategy Box			
Predict	**Summarize**	**Clarify**	**Question**

Write why you think the strategy or strategies you chose
would be helpful.

Predict

_____

_____

Question

_____

_____

Clarify

_____

_____

Summarize

_____

_____

Name _____

REFLECTION

6

What did José and his father learn about each other?

_____

_____

_____

_____

_____

_____

Use these prompts to remind yourself
how to discuss each strategy.

Clarify/Phonics   How to Say a Word

When I come to a word I don't know, first I look for chunks I know.

I know _____. If I still don't know the word, I look for letter

sounds. In this word, I know the sounds ____, ____, and ____. If I

blend the sounds together, the word is _____.

Finally, I check the meaning by rereading the sentence.

Clarify   A Word Meaning

I read this word: _____. I'm not sure what this word

is or what it means. I look at the picture or read to the end of the

sentence. Now I think the word means . . .

Clarify   An Idea

I don't understand this idea: _____.

First I _____ (reread, look at pictures, etc.). Then

I understand that . . . I reread the sentence and it makes sense.

Predict

When I predict, I use clues from the pictures or from what I have read to help me figure out what will happen next (or what I will learn). I predict . . .

Question

When I question, I ask something that can be answered as I read or after I finish reading. I might ask . . .

Summarize

When I summarize, I tell in my own words the important things I have read.

Name _____

Book Log

Title	Author	Date Completed	Comments

Name _____

Book Log

Title	Author	Date Completed	Comments